The Food Truck

Marketing

Handbook

Attract More Customers

Earn Greater Profits!

By Andrew Moorehouse

A Free Gift for You

As a thank you for your purchase, I'm making my book **Food Truck Vehicles and Equipment** available to you for free.

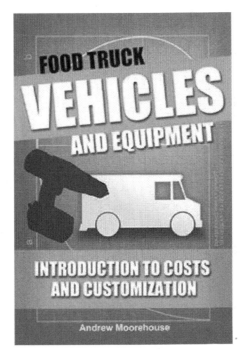

You'll get an introduction to food trucks and the vehicles used in the industry. In this booklet, you can find some basic costs of buying a food truck and learn about what food truck builders can do for you.

Visit the URL below for this exclusive offer:

TheFoodTruckStartup.com/free

Books Available in the Food Truck Startup Series

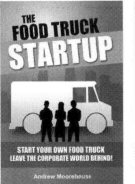

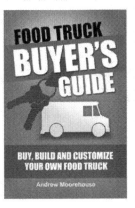

Table of Contents

Introduction

The food truck industry is full of innovation when it comes to marketing and branding. Food truck owners are not only paving the way to new gourmet foods and flavor combinations, they're leading the way to new and creative tactics to get their brands noticed! Try as you might, you won't necessarily see print advertisements or radio and television commercials promoting food trucks... those methods are usually too expensive and outdated in this digital world.

Instead, these new mobile entrepreneurs are utilizing free and low cost tools that are helping grow their customer base and fans! Armed with these extremely effective tools, a food truck owner can now reach massive amounts of followers on smart phones, tablets and computers in an instant! They are in continual contact with their potential customers which helps keep their name fresh in their minds.

In this book, I'll talk about a set of important tools you should be using if you're an established food truck. If you're still in the planning stages and just starting a food truck, you should be setting up these methods now so that they'll be ready when you open for business. Whether you're just starting out or a mobile food veteran, the marketing methods in this book are designed to get you more followers and more customers!

Some of these methods you probably know (there are others you may not be aware of)... But whether you have marketing experience or not, I'm going to help you explore and get to know trusted tools and methods to boost your fan base and eventually your income! Just a quick disclaimer, this book is not necessarily a guide on how to set up your accounts on the various social networks and services. That is because most of the set-up is pretty self-explanatory when you sign up. What this book will do is give you a game plan and strategy to start marketing your food truck online. Let's get started!

-Andrew Moorehouse

Chapter 1 - The Food Truck Brand

Imagine this scenario; Victoria is a graphic designer for a regional insurance company. Her office has 38 employees and is located in a major metropolitan city. The time is 10:04am and by now, she's checked her Twitter and Facebook accounts 3 times for updates. On her 4th check, she sees a Tweet from Cheez Philly, a local food truck announcing they'll be parked near her work at 11am. This is the highlight of Victoria's morning because now she knows where she is going for lunch.

Excited to feast on her favorite Philly cheesesteak sandwich, she sends a Facebook status update to her followers saying where she's going for lunch. Because she has linked her Facebook profile to her Twitter account, that same status update is automatically sent to her Twitter followers as well. Victoria then talks to some co-workers who sit next to her to see if they want to join her for lunch. Because she is subscribed to Cheez Philly's email newsletter, she also gets a message in her Inbox that lists the specials of the day. She forwards this email to a few other co-workers in her company and a few friends who work nearby. By the time lunch rolls around, Victoria has gathered about 5 people she knows to eat at Cheez Philly. They all meet at the truck's location and stand in line. However, the 5 people Victoria knows have brought a few of their friends as well. By the time, they all reach the truck, that one Facebook update and email has generated a total of 9 customers from Victoria! The customer lineup next to Cheez Philly builds quickly and the food truck staff has started to cook furiously!

That's the story of how just one person is able to generate 9 customers to a food truck in one location. The truck owners had sent the same messages to hundreds of other followers so other people in the same area repeated what Victoria did and brought their own friends. This is how social media and food truck marketing works.

Popular Social Media Tools

Food truck marketing is like "digital" word-of-mouth referrals except that these messages can spread quickly and to a lot of people. This is a great time for food truck owners because many of the tools are free or have a very low cost to implement. I'm sure you're aware that Twitter and Facebook are among the most popular marketing platforms for food trucks but there are many other tools mobile food owners should use to gain the edge on their competition.

300 Customers from Tweeting

The pioneer of food trucks, "Kogi BBQ" in Los Angeles were the innovators (at the time) in their use of social media to announce their locations and to get their brand out to the masses.

Because the very nature of food trucks is mobile, they used Twitter to inform their followers where their truck will be and then Tweeted again when their truck arrived. Kogi fans enthusiastically watched their Twitter feeds for the next update from this Korean BBQ taco truck. Their Twitter updates were able to draw 300 to 800 people to a single location! Because of their incredible success, many mobile entrepreneurs have followed in their footsteps. In the following pages, I will be explaining how to use Twitter and Facebook to maximize your marketing plan as well as introduce you to the other effective tools you should be using as part of a complete food truck marketing strategy. These "other" tools have been proven highly effective by marketing experts but have not gained much publicity in the food truck industry. By implementing the strategies listed in this guide, you will be able to rise above the competition and increase your brand awareness, number of followers and ultimately increase sales!

At the end of the book, I will introduce one final tool that will tie together all the methods mentioned in this book to help you generate a flood of social media followers for your truck with only about 30 minutes of work!

Throughout this book I'm going to use a fictitious food truck called "Cheez Philly" to make it easier for you to follow along with my examples. At the time of this writing, there is no truck named Cheez Philly (that I know of). As you follow along in this book, you can replace the name Cheez Philly with your own truck name to make the information more relevant to you! But if you happen to have a food truck named Cheez Philly, well, you have a personalized marketing plan put together just for you!

Chapter 2 - Tweeting Out Loud

Twitter, the online social media and micro-blogging platform was launched in 2006 and quickly gained world-wide popularity for its services. By the beginning of 2012, there were a reported 500 million users generating over 340 Tweets a day! Its popularity could be attributed to the ease of use and the ability to send short messages to a large number of people. Not to mention, the service is also free!

Twitter messages are limited to 140 characters which means your message has to be concise and to the point. You won't be elaborating on a lot of detail when crafting your Tweets but you can still get your point across with those short messages. Twitter also gives you the ability to embed links, photos, conduct public conversations, send private messages, tracking and up to the minute updates.

How to Set Up Your Account

Getting your own Twitter account is super easy! Using your favorite internet browser, go to **www.twitter.com**. When the page opens, there are only 2 things you can do. Sign in as an existing user or sign up as a new user. In this example, we will be signing up as a new user. In the initial step of creating your account, Twitter asks for your full name, email address and password.

Your email and password are pretty straightforward in this step but I want to elaborate a bit more on the box that asks for your full name. Normally if you were using this as your personal account, you'd enter your first and last name. Instead, we'll enter the name of our food truck. Since my example truck is called Cheez Philly, I will enter "Cheez Philly" in the full name box. Click sign up when you're done.

On the next page, you'll be presented with some more account information details. The information I'll focus on here is the username box. This box will display the full name I entered in the sign up screen except that there will be no spaces between words. So I entered "Cheez Philly" for my full name but my username is converted to "CheezPhilly".

An important thing to note is that if someone else already has the username "CheezPhilly", Twitter will automatically add a character to the end of the username. This is usually a number. So if someone already owns the username "CheezPhilly", Twitter will convert my name to "CheezPhilly1". That number could vary depending on how many people already have that name.

If for some reason your username is already taken, you can make changes to it in your account settings. For marketing purposes, I would not want to just let Twitter pick the letters that go after my name if my preferred name wasn't available. So if Twitter told me my username is going to be "CheezPhilly1", I'd change it to one of these combinations:

CheezPhillySanDiego

CheezPhillySD

CheezPhillyFoodTruck

CheezPhillySDFoodTruck

CheezPhillyEats

CheezPhillyTruck

CheezPhillyStreetFood

I could go on and on but you get the idea. I started out by using a city as part of my username because there could be a chance that there is another truck in another city with the same name so you can differentiate yourself with a city name. I've seen several examples of this happening.

Your username will be converted to contact info that you can use to share with your followers. So for Cheez Philly, here's the Twitter contact info I would share with people interested in my truck:

@CheezPhilly

http://twitter.com/CheezPhilly

One more thing, for my username, I used capital letters at the beginning of each word. So instead of using "cheezphilly", I prefer "CheezPhilly". Notice how the second example is easier to read?

Additional Set-Up Tasks

I don't want to go over too many of the initial set-up procedures because Twitter helps you through this step-by-step in the sign up process. However, there are a few additional things I do want to mention. You will want to provide your website address and provide a great description of your business when setting up your account. This information will appear with your profile information when people visit your main Twitter feed page. Mobile phone users will also see this information on their Twitter apps when they tap on your profile name. By providing a good description and your website address, viewers can easily get to your website for more information about your business.

Sending Your First Tweet

Sending Twitter updates is really simple. On the web or on your phone's Twitter app, there will be an icon that looks like a square with a feather coming out of it.

This is the "Compose New Tweet" button. Just click that and type your message. Remember you only have 140 characters to work with so keep it short. One thing that gets you to your character limit faster than anything is adding web addresses. But there will be lots of times you will want to link to your own website or other sites. You can shorten the URLs to reduce the number of characters in your Tweet. Fortunately, Twitter has this ability built-in so you can still post links and compose a decent message at the same time.

Effective Food Truck Tweets

Marketing your food truck with Twitter has many advantages! You want to send out the most effective messages that will drive customers to your truck. So here's a plan of action you can follow to get the best results from your Tweets. Let's say today is Friday and I'm just starting my day. Here's a sequence of Tweets I'd send throughout the day.

8am - "We will be at #BalboaPark today 11am serving up hot cheesesteak sandwiches! Get out today weather is going to be nice!"

8:30am – "Here's the menu for today at #BalboaPark http://ow.ly/cM7A6"

10am – "We're on our way to #BalboaPark serving our delicious cheesesteak sandwiches at 11am. Bring a friend!"

10:45am - "We're just about ready to open at #BalboaPark! Our steak is on the grill!"

11am – "Now serving hot cheesesteak sandwiches at #BalboaPark"

11:45am – "Try our new Jalapeno Cheesesteak Slider at #Balboa Park today! We'll be here until 2pm"

12:15pm – "Our cheesesteak sandwiches are flying out the door! Get yours now at #BalboaPark"

12:30pm – "Here's a shot of one of the cheesesteak sandwiches we're serving at #BalboaPark today http://ow.ly/i/R7vS"

1pm – "We're serving Jalapeno Cheesesteak Sliders for another hour at #BalboaPark"

1:55pm – "Thank you for a wonderful day! We enjoyed meeting each and every one of you!"

7pm – "Our favorite moment of the day! http://ow.ly/cM0A6"

7:30pm – "We won't be at our usual location tomorrow because we're catering a wedding at Coronado Community Center"

Analyzing the Tweet Schedule

Your Tweets won't necessarily follow the exact style or times that I displayed up above but I do want to explain what I'm doing to try and gain customers with each message. You'll probably notice that there are Tweets sent throughout the day. That keeps your followers up to date on what you're doing. Let's analyze each Tweet by time of day.

8am – This Tweet announces early in the day where we'll be and what time we'll be open for business. As an incentive, we tell our followers that the weather will be nice so get outside! We also use the hashtag with #BalboaPark so people searching for Balboa Park will see our messages also.

8:30am – This Tweet lets our followers see our menu to get an idea of what we'll be serving. The link goes to the menu page on the Cheez Philly website.

10am – This Tweet announces that Cheez Philly is on the road and headed to our destination. It also encourages the follower to bring additional people. Nobody likes to eat alone!

10:45am – This Tweet is pretty self-explanatory.

11am – This Tweet announces that Cheez Philly is now open for business at Balboa Park.

11:45am – To entice people to visit us, we entice them by suggesting an item from our menu and let people know how long we'll be at our location.

12:15pm – This Tweet is intended to generate excitement and to keep Cheez Philly on the minds of followers.

12:30pm- In this Tweet, we'll attach an image of one of our sandwiches so our followers can see what we're serving. People eat with their eyes and this will get their stomachs to grumble!

1pm – Again we tell our audience about one of our menu items and how much time they have before we pack up and leave.

1:55pm – By this time, we're about ready to shut down service and we send a Thank You message to everyone.

7pm – Later in the day when we have time, we'll Tweet a photo or two from the day. This can be a photo sent directly through Twitter or we'll include a link to a blog post on the Cheez Philly website which includes the photos.

7:30pm – At the end of the day, we'll announce where we'll be the next day. But in this instance, we inform our followers that we'll be catering an event instead of being at our usual location. We do this because this is a sneaky way to let people know we also do catering.

Whoa! That seems like a lot of Tweeting in a day for a 3 hour service! But it's important to keep your followers informed and on the top of their minds. Before going to the next section, I want to explain a couple more things about the Tweets listed above.

First of all, you'll notice I used the hashtag (#) with Balboa Park. What the hashtag does is help others find information related to a topic. In my Tweet examples above, I used #BalboaPark because that is where Cheez Philly will be located and I wanted people searching for Balboa Park to see that we will be there. It's just another way to make my Tweets reach a wider audience than just my immediate followers. Of course you can add more hashtags but don't go overboard with too many!

Second, you probably noticed that I used a link in my Tweet like this:

http://ow.ly/cM0A6

When you look at this link, it really makes no sense. But, it is a legitimate link that has simply been shortened so that I don't reach my 140 character limit too soon. Most web links are huge which is why they have to be shortened so you'll have room for the rest of your message. Don't worry if that link looks foreign to you now. I will fully explain how to create a link like that in the next section.

Automating Tweets

If you add it up, there are a total of 12 Tweets I've listed to be sent out in a single day. While that may seem like a lot, each one has a specific purpose and helps get your name out there. This can help drive more traffic to your truck, your website and also boost the visibility of your brand name.

You might be wondering how you're going to find the time to Tweet all these messages throughout the day? After all, you still have a business to run and that's going to keep you busy enough without having to think about Tweeting… especially when your truck is operating at the busiest time of the day. The good news is that you can schedule these Tweets ahead of time in one sitting! That is of course your messages are generic enough that people won't be suspicious that they've been pre-scheduled. In the next chapter, I'll explain how you can automate this task so it takes less thought and less time to manage your Twitter updates!

Chapter 3 - Scheduling and Timing Tweets

In the course of your day, you are going to be extremely busy with all aspects of your food truck business. But it just so happens that updating your Twitter status is one of the key tasks to letting people know where your truck will be operating. So how do you send out relevant Tweets without making it feel like another chore to do in your busy schedule?

Fortunately, clever software experts have made scheduling Tweets a possibility! This can have a huge impact on your productivity! The reason scheduling can work for you is that you already know:

Your next location

The time you'll be there

The time you're leaving

The items you're serving

There are pictures of your food

Special events you're attending

Promotional pricing

New items you're offering

Next day's location

Not only that, you probably already know where you're going to be for a full week, 2 weeks even a whole month! So scheduling Tweets makes total sense! If there are locations and times already on your calendar, then you should start scheduling your Tweets right away. The easiest way is to use a service called Hootsuite.

Schedule and Manage Your Social Media

Hootsuite is a free social media management platform that is available on the web from your computer or mobile phone. It does nothing more than to help coordinate all your social media accounts in one place. This can be a powerful tool in your business. It can be used to manage Twitter, Facebook, LinkedIn, Google+ and others.

Linking Hootsuite to your Twitter account is really easy. You just have to have a Twitter account. Once you're linked, you can start using Hootsuite exclusively to send and receive Tweets.

Anything you can to do with Twitter can be done with Hootsuite. You no longer have to go into Twitter anymore. In fact, after I linked my accounts, I hardly ever log into the actual Twitter page or Twitter app on my iPhone anymore!

You can send out Tweets just like before, but now, you'll have the ability to schedule your Tweets and even track clicks from your embedded links.

Hootsuite Scheduler

Scheduling Tweets with Hootsuite is about as easy as sending out a regular Tweet. The only difference is that instead of clicking the "Send Now" button, you will click on a button that looks like a calendar page. When you click the calendar button, a calendar interface will pop-up similar to a calendar you'd see on a commercial airline's booking page. You simply click on the date you want the Tweet to be sent and indicate the time. It's super easy!

Remember that list of 12 Tweets in Chapter 2? Those can easily be scheduled the night before so you don't have to think about it the next day. Those types of messages can be saved in a text document so you can cut and paste into Hootsuite, eliminating the need to type them every night. All you have to do is make slight modifications each time you schedule.

Of course if you ever run into problems like a mechanical failure from your truck, you'll have to go in and delete those scheduled Tweets so your followers won't expect you show up!

URL Shortening and Tracking

Another great feature found in Hootsuite is the ability to shorten and track links in your Tweets. Hootsuite uses their own URL protocol when it shortens links. Their links start with:

http://ow.ly/

Any link you type in can be shortened to save character space when composing Tweets. Hootsuite provides an input box just under the composition window to enter your links for conversion. Once you hit the "Shrink" button, the shortened link is automatically inserted into your Tweet.

The other great thing about shrinking your links is that now they can be tracked by Hootsuite. This information can be valuable if you need to know how many people are clicking your links to get to your website or other places on the internet. Each shortened URL is unique with a statistics page at Hootsuite to show all the links you've embedded into Tweets. You may or may not need this feature but its there for you to use!

Chapter 4 - Facebook

The next most popular social media tool for food truck owners is Facebook. Facebook is another free tool that shares some similar functionality to Twitter. However, there are certain features in Facebook that are perfect for promoting your food truck. Yes, you can post status updates like Twitter but you are not limited to 140 characters.

But let's take a small step back before we talk about actually using Facebook for promotion. First of all, you need to set up a personal Facebook account. Getting a Facebook account is much like setting up your Twitter account so I'm not going to go into too much detail about that here. Their website can walk you step-by-step through the sign up process. Chances are you already have a personal Facebook account that you use with friends and family. That is great! However, I do not recommend using your personal account for your business!

Instead, you'll need to set up a fan page strictly for your food truck. This is usually tied to your personal Facebook account but they are independent of each other. A fan page should be used for business because it is viewable by the public and can be found directly through a web search.

When you create your fan page, you will be presented with a number of categories to classify your business. The natural tendency for food truck owners is to select "Local Business or Place". While that seems like a perfect fit, I don't recommend that category for food trucks. Instead, choose "Company, Organization or Institution" or "Brand or Product". Either one of these categories are perfect for mobile food businesses.

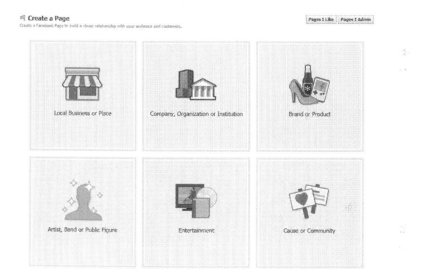

While it is true that a food truck is a local business, you don't necessarily have a street address that would be associated with your truck or even regular business hours. You'll be in different locations all the time at different times of the day! When you choose "Local Business or Place", Facebook will ask you to fill out address input boxes for this type of information. The address and hours of operation information will show up at the top of your Facebook page near your profile image. The only reason why a mobile food owner would classify their truck as a "Local Business or Place" would be if they also own a catering company or restaurant and have an actual physical address where people can personally visit during business hours.

However, if you already have a fan page for your truck and you previously set it up as a "Local Business or Place", you have the ability (as an administrator) to go in and change it to one of the classifications I mentioned above.

First Impressions on Your Facebook Page

When people visit your Facebook page, the first thing they're going to see is your cover photo. Visitors can't miss it because it's the largest image at the top of the screen. It almost covers the whole width of the Facebook window. You want something compelling and unique for this image! This image should shout out what your food truck is all about!

Maybe you could insert a photo of your truck if you have some stunning graphics to show off. Another idea would be to put a clean version of your logo there... but there's a better place for your logo as I'll explain later. Lastly, you could insert a beautiful image of one of your signature dishes to make people hungry when they visit your page. Just remember that this main image should spark some sort of reaction or make an impression with your visitors.

Technically speaking, this image should be 851x315 pixels at 72dpi (dots per inch) and in JPEG format. The file size should be 100kb or less. If you create an image that does not fit those pixel dimensions, your picture will appear distorted or won't fit the allotted area in the cover photo window. An image of 851x315 can be created easily in Photoshop. If you don't have Photoshop, a free image editing tool (almost) as good as Photoshop is GIMP. Cover photos can come from your existing Facebook photos or you can simply upload a new photo from your computer.

Next, you'll want to upload a profile picture. This is a much smaller image that rests towards the lower left-hand corner of your cover image. Your profile picture represents your page on other parts of Facebook, advertisements, sponsored stories and news feeds. You could use almost any image for your profile picture but I recommend using a logo. This is because Facebook users are going to identify you with this particular image throughout the site. If you already use a Gravatar for your business, I'd recommend using the same image as your Gravatar image.

The size of your Facebook profile image needs to be 180x180 pixels. This is the maximum size of the profile image on your main Facebook page. However, this image needs to be scalable down to 32x32 pixels! Why 32x32? This is the size of your profile image when it appears in news feeds. You can check how your image will look by scaling (shrinking) your image in Photoshop or GIMP to see if it is still readable at the smaller 32x32 image size.

Information about Your Business

This next part should not be neglected because it will help your Facebook visitors to easily find out more about your business and how they can get in contact with you. I've seen numerous food truck Facebook pages where the owners only filled out minimal information about their business making it frustrating when the information is missing. Keep in mind that a lot of people are going to first learn about you on Facebook and you want to create good first impression. Here are some of the information boxes you can fill out for your profile:

Address

About

Description

Mission

Founded

Awards

Products

Phone

Email

Website

If I were to pick the most important fields to really elaborate on… I'd choose:

About

Description

Products

When filling out the About section, it's a good idea to write a short description and end with your website address. Why include your website address? These words will appear right below your profile image with an active link to your website. Here's an example:

Crunchy cheesy sandwiches grilled to delicious perfection on the streets of San Diego! We are www.cheezphilly.com.

There's not much room for the description so keep it short. You might have to play around with the length of this text for it all to fit under your profile image. But depending on the category you choose, the About text may or may not show up in this spot. If you choose "Local Business or Place" then information about your hours of operation and location will appear here instead.

Setting Up Your Description

The Description section is where you should share complete and detailed information about your mobile food business. You're not doing your business any favors when you neglect these sections. People are on your page because they want to find out more about your company!

Then in the Products section, you can list out some of your most popular dishes and give a short description so readers can get an idea of what's in these menu items.

The last things you definitely need to fill out are your Phone, Email and Website information. This allows visitors to contact you with questions. Usually, the reason people call or email is to find out whether you do catering or not. So you need to share your contact info here. And by the way, please answer any legitimate questions. I've seen many complaints on blogs and websites where a potential customer has left a negative comment because they were never able to get in touch with a mobile food owner or they never received a reply back. These comments can be seen by everyone and may have a negative effect if they see that you don't communicate back to people's questions.

Finally, fill in your website address so you can direct visitors to your site where you will have more details about your food truck. The website address will show up on your About page and is an active link for readers to click through to your site.

Chapter 5 - Your Facebook Status

You already know that Facebook can be used much like Twitter to update your status and to let people know what's going on with your business.

But did you know that you can also pin one of your Facebook updates to the top of your fan page for up to 7 days using the "Pin to the top" function? This is handy when you want to highlight an update temporarily. To pin an update, just click on the pencil icon with a pop up that says Edit or Remove. Click on the pop up and then click "Pin to the top". An update that has been "pinned" can be identified by a small orange flag in the upper right hand corner of the post.

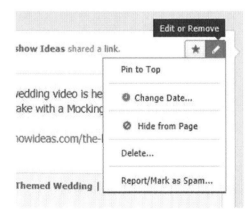

After 7 days, the "pinned" post will return to its normal place in your timeline. But what if you don't need your post highlighted for the full 7 days? You can pin for shorter than 7 days by manually "unpinning" the post when it becomes old news. This can be done by reversing the pinning process.

Why "Pin" a Status Update?

Normally, status updates on Facebook drop down the timeline each time you add a new update. But there are times you will want to "Pin" an update so that it stays at the top of the list. For example, Cheez Philly just got booked at the San Diego International Car Show event. This car show is a three day event and Cheez Philly is going to be there all three days. This means Friday, Saturday and Sunday.

Because the default duration of a pinned update is 7 days, I'll post an update on Monday on my Facebook page that goes something like this:

"Cheez Philly is going to be at the San Diego International Car Show Dec 27th-30th from 11am to 4pm daily. Come see hot cars, say hi and enjoy special prices on our gourmet Philly cheesesteak sandwiches! Look for the big cheesy yellow truck near the entrance. Like this comment and let others know we'll be there!"

After I post this message, I could pin it and leave it as is and let it expire on Sunday because I've back-timed 7 days from when I want it to disappear from the top of my fan page. That would be easy and I'd only have to post it once and I don't have to do anything more with it after the event.

However, I could unpin the post on Friday morning which is the first day of the car show and replace it with a new message that says this:

"Cheez Philly is at the San Diego International Car Show today from 11am to 4pm. Come see hot cars, say hi and enjoy special prices on our gourmet Philly cheesesteak sandwiches! Look for the big cheesy yellow truck near the entrance. Like this comment and let others know we'll be there!"

In the 2nd post, I slightly changed the text to reflect a more current message that says something to the effect that we are at the car show from 11am to 4pm today. See the difference? I would pin this update starting on the day of the event and then manually unpin it sometime on Sunday night after the car show is over.

Additional Fan Page Tips

I know you know how to post updates on Facebook but I want to give you some additional information to make your posts more likely to be read by your followers. In the above examples, notice how I ended the update with the line "Like this comment and let others know we'll be there!"

This encourages people to take action and click the "Like" button for this post. Liking something on Facebook is easy and there's nothing wrong with politely asking your readers to do so. Here's the reason why you want a person to like your update. When they click "Like", your message will appear in the news feed of their friends' pages and create more exposure for your message.

Creating Eye-Catching Updates

Typing text based messages is just part of the strategy of marketing your food truck on Facebook. To make your posts really stand out, you should try to insert an image on as many posts as you can. I'd recommend on every post if possible. This is easy to do if you carry a small digital camera or a smart phone around with you.

The reason I recommend uploading an image on your posts is because it takes up more space on the Facebook page and people are more prone to look at images than read text. In fact, images can prompt your followers to read your text when they might have easily skipped over it. So take pictures as often as you can so you'll have a library of images ready.

Insert pictures or graphic designs of anything related to your business. This can include:

Truck Images

Truck Graphics

Food Images

Close-Ups of Ingredients

Business Card in Hand

Truck Logo

Employees

Mascots

Special Guests

Customer Line-Up

Event Pictures

Etc.

I'm sure you get the idea! You should insert any image that is relevant to what you're saying in your post to get people to look at your message. If you're on the Facebook website, just click on the Add Photo/Video button at the top of the Update Status box. If you're uploading from your phone, click "Status" then click on the icon that looks like a camera. From there, click "Take Photo or Video" or the "Choose From Library" button.

Add Video Clips

Not only can you insert still images, you can also insert video clips into your Facebook posts. I recommend doing this also. With smart phones and digital cameras that can shoot HD video, it's easier than ever to add a video to your post. Videos draw attention to your post just like images do because the thumbnail shows up like an image. But videos can be more engaging and can tell a story better than in a still image.

Most of the video you will insert will be short and uncut shots… unless you want to spend the time to edit some clips together before you upload them. If this is the case, then I'd suggest uploading the edited video clip to your YouTube account and then embedding the YouTube link into your Facebook post. Just type out your message first and then copy the YouTube web address of the video and paste it at the end of your post.

The linked video will show up as an extra content box directly below your post. This also makes your post larger and more visible to people looking through their timeline. I'll have more about YouTube in a later chapter.

Add Website Links

If you have a website and have a blog on it, then you should also be adding links to your site for all your new blog posts. Use this feature to get people to your site so they can get more information about your activities or share information that is only available on your site!

Once visitors are on your site, you can get them to view your menu, learn more about you, make comments on your blog, email with questions, enter contests, sign up for a mailing list, etc.

Adding a link to your site in your Facebook updates is easy. Just copy the website address, type your message in the status box and then paste your website address at the end of your message. The linked site will appear in a content box directly below your post. Just like I did with sharing a photo or video, adding a web link also makes your post larger and more visible to people looking through their timeline.

You also have the ability to choose the thumbnail image that appears with your link. Your choices depend on how many pictures are embedded on that particular web page. Not every image is going to be relevant so it's good that Facebook gives you the option to choose your image instead of automatically selecting it for you.

Chapter 6 - Email Marketing

For years, successful marketers have used email to help promote products, companies, events, and more! Email marketing is an extremely effective way to get your message directly to your customers. However, in the past, some abused this strategy and thus, the term Spam was born. Even with this tarnished reputation, email marketing still remains a viable and cost-effective way to reach customers.

When I say cost-effective, you'll have to realize that good email marketing services are not free like Twitter and Facebook. But it does offer opportunities that the free social media tools don't have. I know you might be saying, "Why should I spend money on email marketing when I can use Twitter and Facebook for free?"

Social Media Facts

Let's start out with fascinating statistics about internet usage, social media networks and the number of people that actually utilize them.

The fact of the matter is that NOT everyone uses Twitter or Facebook. According to statistics gathered by the Pew Research Center in 2011, 77% of American adults use the internet. Out of those people, 92% use email while only 61% use online social media.

Facebook clearly has a lot of users... Over 500,000,000 and counting! However, only about 50% will log in on a given day. If you're sending out messages on Facebook about your truck locations, realize that a lot of people are going to miss out on your updates.

This is true for Twitter as well. Twitter has over 20,000,000 users with 500,000+ users signing up daily. But only 8% of Americans over the age of 12 are actually using Twitter.

We are asked to Follow, Like, Tweet, Share and Link on a daily basis. News programs, TV shows, non-profit organizations, restaurants and just about any other organization has placed Twitter and Facebook icons on their advertisements, business cards, signage and more asking us to be part of their social network. You can like or share these organization's messages but they are not very personable.

It would be easier and more reliable to get these messages delivered straight to a person's Inbox. For example, if Victoria was on the Cheez Philly mailing list, she might receive the current week's schedule in her email and she would more likely forward that to other people she knows. And chances are she'd include a nice personalized message from her inviting others to join her when the truck is near her work. The same thing would be harder to do with Twitter and Facebook considering that Tweets are limited to 140 characters and Facebook updates can't be forwarded like an email.

This is why status updates are done on a daily basis. But a huge opportunity is missed by not being able to share a longer message to your followers. So in addition to sharing the week's schedule, our fictional food truck Cheez Philly could also highlight a new menu item, include detailed information about an upcoming event, promote giveaways and more!

Email Segmentation

By having an email list, you can even segment customers by zip code or other factors specified in your sign-up form. This form can be easily added to your website to capture subscriber information. By possessing this detailed information, you could choose to only email those subscribers that live or work near the area you will be located on any given day. I'm not necessarily saying you should segment like this but I wanted to give you an idea of what is possible with your email list. Twitter and Facebook doesn't allow you to do this type of segmentation. Paid Facebook ads could help you target certain customers but I don't really recommend it because it can be costly!

So don't limit your digital marketing plan by strictly using Twitter and Facebook. I'm here to open your eyes to a method long used by marketing professionals that is proven to work. Why do you think companies like Amazon, Groupon, Living Social, Southwest Airlines and others want you to sign up for their emails? These companies know email marketing is effective and it generates results!

Implementing an Email List

Adding an email subscription form to your website is as easy as pasting a line of code in a designated area of your site. If you know how to embed a YouTube video on your site, you can insert an email subscription form. The email form is often called an opt-in form because subscribers need to "opt-in" to receive your messages. And this doesn't just mean that subscribers enter their email address and hit send. New subscribers must double opt-in. The double opt-in was made mandatory by the CAN-SPAM Act of 2003.

What the CAN-SPAM Act mandated was to require that all new email subscribers to first enter their email address into an online form (and other info if needed) and then submit their information to a website owner. Immediately, the subscriber would get an email requiring the subscriber to confirm that they indeed want to subscribe to the newsletter. They would have to click a confirmation link in order to be added to the newsletter. This is the double opt-in. It's really not a big deal but is legally required by law. Don't worry, this part is completely automated so don't think you have to constantly monitor this activity!

In fact, once you have your email opt-in form on your website, a lot of it can be automated! Before I go any further, I'll tell you that my preferred email marketing service is AWeber.

AWeber fully complies with the CAN-SPAM Act so you can stay legal in your email marketing activities. This is the service I use with all of my websites and it is easy to use. If you use an email service that does not require double opt-in, then ultimately, you are not abiding by the law when you collect email addresses.

Create Your Own Newsletter

When you have a service like AWeber, you can send out instant email messages just like you'd do with social media. These can be location updates for the day or the week. However, when you use AWeber, you definitely will want to utilize their autoresponder features. The autoresponder essentially sends out a series of pre-written emails at pre-determined intervals. This is ideal for creating a newsletter for your food truck business. The newsletter can be a powerful relationship building tool to engage your customers.

These pre-written emails should contain "evergreen" content meaning they should not mention anything that is relevant to a date or time of year. That's because these emails will be sent out automatically starting at the point the subscriber signs up. So every subscriber will get the same series of emails you've written but everyone receives them at different times. The purpose of these autoresponder messages is to get the subscriber used to receiving your emails and to be able to offer a newsletter about your truck on autopilot. Just so you know the autoresponder messages in AWeber are called "Follow Up" messages.

Using my example truck Cheez Philly, the subject lines of the "Follow Up" messages could be formulated like this:

Day 1 – Welcome to the Cheez Philly Newsletter

Day 2 – About Cheez Philly

Day 4 – Chef Andrew Cooks a Mean Cheesesteak

Day 7 – How Cheez Philly Got Started

Week 2 – Our Farm Fresh Ingredients

Week 3 – Meet the Cheez Philly Staff

Week 5 –Custom Catering with Cheez Philly

Week 7 – Cheez Philly is on Twitter

Week 9 – Order Your Cheez Philly T-Shirts

Month 3 – We Love Our Cheesy Customers!

Month 4 – San Diego's Best Food Truck

Month 5 – We'll Make Your Special Event Cheesy!

Month 6 – Look Stylish in our Cheez Philly T-Shirts

I just listed subject lines for six months' worth of autoresponder emails. Think you can do that? These emails don't have to be long but as your customers receive each message, your company and your brand will stay fresh in their minds.

Notice in the beginning, the intervals between emails are shorter. But as time goes on, I start spacing them out further until I only send one a month. This is to prevent the newsletter subscriber from feeling like they are getting too many emails from me. Also notice that I included a couple of emails offering Cheez Philly t-shirts. So if you have merchandise you sell, they can be promoted in these emails. The subject of your emails can be anything you want but you can use my example when you start your own email newsletter.

And just to reiterate, the best thing about the autoresponder newsletter is that it is completely automated! You could spend half a day composing your messages and once they've been successfully integrated into AWeber's autoresponder, you don't have to touch it again unless you need to make modifications. In my examples, I could essentially use those pre-written emails for the life of the Cheez Philly food truck. You could do the same for yours!

Scheduling One-Time Messages

Now that we have some newsletter content flowing automatically, let's look at the one-time email updates you can send out. In AWeber, these messages are called "Broadcast" emails. Broadcast emails are used to deliver more timely information like truck locations, times, daily specials, etc.

For example, on Monday morning, Cheez Philly would send out the week's schedule listing locations and times in the email. The beauty of this email schedule is that this message can stay in a person's Inbox all week so they can go back and check your locations without having to go to Twitter or Facebook. They can also forward this email to several people and those recipients can subsequently forward that message to even more people. Email is often more convenient for people because some companies don't allow their employees to surf the web.

You can also send out immediate changes to your schedule. Say for example, Cheez Philly got a last minute booking to a celebrity party and had to cancel a scheduled location. A "Broadcast" message could be sent out indicating the cancellation and can also explain why. This message would more likely be received by email subscribers than through social media simply because emails are often perceived as more important than information gathered through social media.

It's important to note that a "Broadcast" message can be sent immediately or scheduled in AWeber. Scheduling your emails can also help you save time and automate your email marketing strategy. Let's say you have a special announcement about your truck's one year anniversary. You already know which day that is going to be so you can write a message (or several messages) ahead of time and schedule them to go out on the days and time you want. This will help you save valuable time! By being able to do this in one writing session, you won't have to think about it later.

If you want to try out email marketing for your food truck business, you can use the link below to access a month of AWeber's service for $1. In this 30 day period, you can create all your autoresponders, broadcast messages, sign-up forms and all the other services that AWeber members enjoy.

foodtruckbusinessplan.com/Aweber

It's worth trying out especially if you've never used an autoresponder service before. Email marketing is the secret weapon used by all major companies to communicate with their customers. I recommend that you build a small campaign and implement it on your site so you can see all the steps involved in creating an autoresponder sequence. If you find it works for your business, you can build upon your initial campaign or revise the messages easily. Any message saved in your account can be revised or copied and used as a template.

What I've learned from email marketing experts is that you should implement an email subscription form on your website as soon as you can to start capturing email addresses early on. See how many subscribers you can get in the first month. Just cancel within 30 days to get a refund on your dollar.

However, email marketing takes time to acquire quality email addresses. By quality, I mean getting email addresses from people who will actually buy from you. The next chapter will explain simple tactics to get people to sign up to your list. And you'll definitely want to read through to the end of the book for the ultimate strategy to gain email addresses quickly!

Chapter 7 - How to Grow Your Email Subscriber List

Lots of website owners have email subscription forms on their sites asking people to sign up for updates. But there's no information about what people can expect when they subscribe. I've seen numerous examples where there is just a box to enter an email address and a button to join a newsletter. While this will get some subscribers, there is really no incentive for people to sign up. You need to offer something like a gift or giveaway as a reward for joining your newsletter. Just so I'm clear, this is usually something that is free.

Free software demos, training courses, coupons, ebooks and more have been used to entice people to sign up to newsletters on websites. For the food truck industry, I believe an ebook is a perfect giveaway. An ebook is easy to write and people love them! But what kind of ebook do you offer?

The Ebook Giveaway

You could offer an ebook on any topic but keep it relevant to your business. One idea would be to write about your truck and the story of how you got started. Include the history and inspiration it took to start your business. While that can be interesting, another idea is to offer a recipe book of some of your most popular items. You don't have to include too many recipes but keep it at a number you're comfortable with. Maybe 2 to 4 recipes would be sufficient and you could supplement your recipe book with the story of how your truck got started.

I would describe your giveaway as an exclusive recipe book available only to subscribers. This is a highly effective strategy used by seasoned email marketing experts. People usually can't resist free giveaways especially if they find value in it. You might be worried that someone might copy your recipes and either start a food truck to compete with yours or use your recipes and never buy from you again. Chances are that these people will never actually prepare your recipes let alone start their own food truck just because they got a free ebook from you. The main thing is that you captured their email address so you can contact them directly with your promotional messages.

Creating Your Free Ebook

Your ebook giveaway doesn't have to be fancy. You can write it in Microsoft Word, add a few pictures, insert a few links to your website, Facebook and Twitter pages then convert it to a PDF. A book of 7 to 15 pages would be sufficient but you can do any length you want. I suggest making it at least 7 pages.

Format the document so that the text looks attractive and organized. Add graphics and logos so your branding is consistent between all your media. Because an ebook is not a physical object, you really can't show the product because you can't take a picture of it. What do you show on your website to visually represent your book? This is where an ebook cover comes in.

You could make a simple looking cover with MS Paint but I'd recommend Photoshop if you have it. If not, you can download GIMP for free. GIMP is a great Photoshop alternative that has a lot of the features of Photoshop. You can find the download link at:

www.gimp.org

If you are a Photoshop user, you can easily create an ebook cover that looks like this:

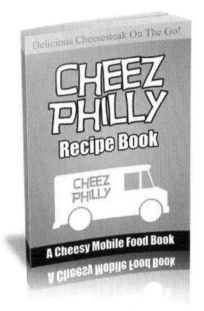

This cover was generated with a set of premium Photoshop actions. These actions are a set of instructions that tells Photoshop how to recreate a project that was created by another user. You can find the exact premium Photoshop actions used for the cover above at:

eBookCoverActions.com

The design phase of the book took the most time... maybe 10 to 15 minutes. But, to render it out to the 3D looking book displayed above literally takes seconds with Photoshop actions. A nice looking cover can go a long way to create credibility and the perception that you are offering a quality giveaway.

Assembling the Subscription Form

Once you have your AWeber account set up, an ebook written and an ebook cover made it's time to put it all together and start collecting email addresses. AWeber has an easy to use visual editor that allows you to drag and drop elements into the subscription form. They have pre-built templates for your email messages. If you end up using a template, I'd recommend a simple design that matches your website's color scheme.

At the top of the subscription form, you should have an image of your ebook. Next, you will want some copy that tells the reader what you want them to do. You could say something like this.

"Download a FREE copy of our famous Cheesesteak recipe book plus join our cheesy newsletter!"

Following the text will be the boxes where people can enter their information. You can capture email addresses, phone numbers, first and last names, zip codes, physical addresses and more. But I recommend keeping this all very simple and only ask for an email address. The simpler you can make it, the more likely people will sign up.

The last element in the subscription form is the Submit button. AWeber allows you to customize the look and the text inside the button. In the example above, I typed the words "Download Now!" as a call to action. When the subscription form is ready, AWeber gives you a simple line of code you need to copy and paste into your website. I'll explain how to do this in the next chapter about websites.

Chapter 8 - Building a Website Yourself

Your website is an essential element of your marketing plan. If you don't have a website these days, you're missing out on the ability to let customers get information about you 24 hours a day. Businesses can spend a decent part of their startup budget on a web designer. But if you haven't hired a designer to build your website yet, I would suggest that you build it yourself!

That's right! Build it yourself! Don't worry if you don't have any coding skills. It's easier to do than you think! Lots of technically challenged people are starting their own websites with WordPress. WordPress is a free content management system that has changed the way websites are built and maintained. Originally designed for blogging, WordPress has evolved to become the standard management platform for a large percentage of websites on the internet today. It is available for free on all hosting plans that offer it.

In the old days when I had to get into the HTML code to update my site, I would end delaying my site updates for years just because it was so cumbersome to do. Now with WordPress, I can update my websites daily with ease. If you know how to use Facebook, you can figure out how to use WordPress. But before I go any further with the website itself, let's discuss domain names and hosting.

Choosing a Domain and Web Hosting

The first step in the creation of your website is picking a domain name. This is also known as a URL or website address. The most popular extensions for domain names are:

.com

.net

.org

Obviously choose a .com as your first choice. So for our fictional food truck, Cheez Philly I'd choose:

CheezPhilly.com

That's perfect if the domain is available and not taken by someone else. But what should you do if your preferred domain is not available? I've seen several cases where there are food trucks in different cities with the same names. In this case, you could go with the .net or .org extensions. But if another truck exists with an identical name as yours, then you should localize your domain with your city or area and stick with a .com extension.

For example, Cheez Philly is based in San Diego but what if I found that there was another Cheez Philly in Philadelphia and they already own CheezPhilly.com? Here is what I could do with my domain name:

CheezPhillyTruck.com

CheezPhillySD.com

CheezPhillySanDiego.com

CheezPhillyFoodTruck.com

CheezPhillyMobile.com

CheezPhillyEats.com

Most trucks have pretty unique names so you're likely to choose an available name. But again, I have seen several cases where two trucks in different parts of the country have the same name.

Once you have a domain name, you will need hosting. A hosting account is where all the files for your website will be stored. I host my websites on Bluehost. They're amazingly affordable and you can get your domain name for free when you sign up using this link:

foodtruckbusinessplan.com/Bluehost

Bluehost also has something called SimpleScripts which allows you to install WordPress with just a few clicks. Once you run SimpleScripts for WordPress, your website will be installed and ready! It really is easy! I've done this with more than 20 websites and have seen people with no website experience successfully build their own sites.

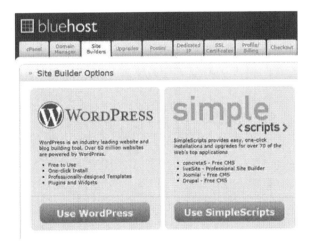

They've made it so easy that almost anyone can do it. It's almost crazy to hire a designer to do the same thing that might take you 15 minutes to do on your laptop in a coffee shop! Most designers are going to create a website in WordPress anyways so why pay them for this process?

Ok, you might be thinking, "Now what? How am I going to make my website look professional?" Well WordPress works with themes which is basically the style and look of your site. After your initial installation of WordPress, your site already has a nice default theme applied to it and is a fully functioning website that is ready for you to add content.

Designing a Beautiful Website

The beauty of using WordPress to manage your website is that there are thousands of free themes available for you to use. WordPress has its own library of themes that can be installed right from the admin panel of your site. Changing the look of your site is super easy. Just search, install and activate a new theme. Have I convinced you that you don't need to hire a web designer to build your site?

And in the slim chance that you can't find a free theme among the thousands in the WordPress directory, you can buy premium themes that are a bit more customized. But the free themes are just as good as any of the paid themes. The difference is that the paid themes may offer some special features not found in the free ones.

If you decide that you need a premium theme, then Woo Themes has a great selection at a great price. At the time of this writing, you can all their themes for about $100. They have a monthly subscription but according to their policies, they allow you to subscribe for one month, download all 94 of their themes and then cancel the subscription. They are continually adding themes so by the time you get to the Woo Themes site, there may be more than 94 premium themes you can download. You can use this link to get all the Woo Themes on their site:

foodtruckbusinessplan.com/WooThemes

Just so you know a single premium theme can cost $50 to $100+ each so the cost of one month of Woo Themes is an incredible savings! The themes are beautiful and you can try out as many as you like after you download their entire collection!

Blogging Made Easy

WordPress was initially created as a blogging platform but it can do a lot more with it today. Those great blogging features are still at the core of this software. That's important because you will most likely want a blog to go along with your website for reader engagement and to update your fans about what you're doing.

To add a blog post, all you have to do is click the Add New Post button and start typing. Your blog posts can contain text, images and embedded video from sites like YouTube. Make sure you have a good catchy title and then add some relevant keywords before you hit the Publish button.

The blogging feature allows you to create a chronological account of your food truck adventures. Every time you post an article, you should also announce it on Facebook and Twitter.

Static Web Pages

For a food truck website, you probably don't want the blog section to be the first thing people see when they visit your site. In WordPress, you can assign a static page to be your home page. A static page is like a blog post but does not appear in the blog timeline. Static pages are what you use to create pages like Home, About, Contact, Menu, FAQ, etc. Buttons for these pages also appear in the navigation bar of your site. The great thing about WordPress is that these buttons are automatically created for you in the navigation bar when you add a page. You can also customize the navigation bar to include any buttons you want including custom button labels.

WordPress Plugins

Plugins allow you to enjoy extra functionality that isn't already built into WordPress. There's probably a plugin for almost anything you want to do. But don't go crazy and install too many plugins because they can slow down your site.

Among the great plugins available, here are a few plugins I recommend as starters for any WordPress based site.

All-In-One SEO Pack – This plugin helps optimize your site and individual pages for search engine optimization

Growmap Anti Spambot Plugin – This plugin will help reduce the amount of spam comments in your blog posts.

Google Analytics for WordPress – Use this plugin to easily insert your Google Analytics tracking code so you can get statistics of your visitors and traffic numbers. For this plugin to function, you need a free Google Analytics account.

XML Sitemap Generator – This plugin allows the search engines to see a complete snapshot of your website so it can be indexed more efficiently. It also notifies search engines when you add more content to your site such as a new blog post.

Digg Digg – This plugin will add a floating social share bar on your site with customizable buttons for all the social networking services including Facebook, Twitter, Google+, StumbleUpon and more.

Contact Form 7 – This plugin automatically creates an email contact form on any page of your website. It includes the ability to prevent spammers from spamming your email Inbox by requiring a Captcha code that a user needs to type in before sending an email message to you. This is ideally incorporated into a Contact page on your website.

Pinterest "Pin It" Button – This plugin places a "Pin It" button on your website's pages that allows visitors to easily click and pin a photo from your page. Configuration is easy by check-marking the settings you want.

Those are the seven basic plugins I'd install right from the start. They're all free and available directly from your WordPress plugins dashboard when you're logged into your site. Later, you might find that you need some custom functionality and that's when you can seek out additional plugins. WordPress has its own directory of thousands of free plugins. But again, if you don't find one in the free directory, you can find a premium plugin elsewhere.

WordPress.com vs. WordPress.org

This is a bit of a confusing subject for most people starting out with WordPress. Everything discussed so far relates to WordPress.org and self-hosted websites. That means installing WordPress on your own internet host and owning your own domain name. The actual website, WordPress.org is where all the support, plugins, themes and other material related to hosting your own WordPress website are found.

WordPress.com is a little bit different. When you go to WordPress.com, you can sign up for a free website that is hosted on the WordPress servers. It's a free online service. You can build a website just like I described before but there are some noticeable differences when you use a WordPress.com site. One of the main differences is in your domain name. If I were to build a free website on WordPress.com, my website address would be:

www.cheesephilly.WordPress.com

That doesn't look very professional and it's hard to remember. Another disadvantage of using WordPress.com is that you don't have the flexibility to add third party plugins, premium themes or coding customizations to your site. You'll be limited to what WordPress offers in their library and bound by their rules. You also don't own your site on WordPress.com.

With that said, I do however recommend that you still create a free WordPress.com site so you can use the WordPress.com Stats plugin that comes with every self-hosted WordPress installation. This plugin is part of a set of WordPress tools called Jetpack.

Website Traffic

As with all websites, it is important to know how many visitors your website is attracting. There are some complicated tools out there that SEO professionals use but I recommend using WordPress.com Stats. This is a very simple plugin that tells you how many visitors are visiting your site each day. It also keeps track of the keywords people are using to find your website. This plugin also tracks the links people are clicking on your site.

For example, if you have links to your Twitter or Facebook pages, you might want to know how many people are actually clicking on those links.

You can also see where the source of your traffic comes from. WordPress.com Stats will show if your visitors came from Google, Facebook, and Twitter or wherever they clicked a link to get to your site.

Activating WordPress.com Stats

To activate the WordPress.com Stats plugin on your self-hosted WordPress site, you need a free WordPress.com website. You need to be logged in to both the free site and your own self-hosted site. The stats plugin is located in the Jetpack module of the admin screen. All you have to do is click on WordPress.com Stats and click to establish a connection from your self-hosted site to the free WordPress.com site. Your sites will be linked in a few seconds and the stats plugin will start working.

It may take two or three days after activation before any data will be shown. The two sites will still be independent of each other but the stats plugin just needs a link to the WordPress.com servers to function.

More Sophisticated Site Analytics

The WordPress.com Stats plugin is usually enough traffic information for most website owners but if you want more detailed and professional website data, you need Google Analytics. Here are some of the things Google Analytics will show you.

Total Visitors

Unique Visitors

Traffic Sources

Exit Data

Demographics

Worldwide Traffic Origins

Average Visitor Time

And there are a lot more data they track that I won't list here. But if you're in charge of marketing your website, this data can be invaluable. Google Analytics is free. When you sign up, they will assign you a unique Google Analytics code that you have to place in the coding of your website. This is usually in the PHP files in the header or footer. Hopefully that doesn't deter you from using this awesome service. Remember back when I was discussing plugins? If you installed the Google Analytics for WordPress plugin, adding this code to your site is a snap!

If you have a Google Analytics account, just make sure the analytics plugin on your site is activated and then paste the tracking code into the plugin that you copied from Google Analytics. Google then needs to verify that you indeed own your site and then it will start collecting the data from you. Again, it could take several days for any statistics to show up.

You Can Build Your Own Website

I hope I have explained enough so that you can feel confident in building your own website. Realistically, you can build your own self-hosted website for less than $100. Compare that with hiring a web designer that will basically do exactly what I explained in this chapter but he or she could charge you 10 times as much or more!

I've also seen advertisements on television from companies that sell website services to businesses. I would recommend against using those services. They have high monthly fees and you don't own the website. Once you stop paying, your site is removed. Hosting on your own gives you many more options... the least of which is that you own your site and can do whatever you want with it!

And here are some shocking numbers, getting your own web host and domain costs less than $100 a year but those other services seen on television can run $40-$50 or more a month! In the food truck business where being cost-effective is everything, building and hosting your own website is really the best way to go!

Lastly, one of the great things about Bluehost is that you can host an unlimited number of websites on a single hosting account. That means for the same monthly fee, you can run 1 or more websites without buying extra hosting plans. So if you own more than one business or want to have personal websites for each member of your family, you can do it with one Bluehost account. You can also install WordPress for free on each of these sites. The only thing you need to do for the additional websites is to buy a domain name for each one. All additional sites will operate independently of each other and is really the most economical choice!

Chapter 9 - YouTube Marketing

Online video can be a powerful tool for marketing your food truck. Video can convey messages and emotions that can't be replicated in writing. In a world where the majority of phones and digital cameras have the ability to shoot HD video, it's easy to capture video wherever you might be! Along with your website, a YouTube channel can help sell your services and gain more customers.

Here's a little background information on YouTube. Did you know that YouTube is the 2nd largest search engine in the world? What about this? Did you know that Google, the number one search engine also owns YouTube? Those are 2 compelling reasons to get on YouTube. You see, YouTube videos show up prominently on Google searches. The more videos you have, the better your visibility on Google.

Starting a YouTube channel is easy and it's free. But there are a few things you should know before you start posting videos.

Your YouTube Channel

When you create your YouTube channel, you want to give it the same name as your truck. I will call my channel CheezPhilly. But if that name is taken, I'll have to come up with an alternate name like I explained in the last chapter. So if CheezPhilly is already taken, I'd call it CheezPhillySD or something like that. Here's how my channel name will appear to visitors on YouTube.

CheezPhilly's Channel

The channel name is one continuous word so when you have more than one word to your name, I'd advise that you use capital letters for the first letter in each word of your username. If not, here's how my channel could be displayed:

cheezphilly's Channel

Just to make this clear, here's an example from Nom Nom Truck's YouTube channel. They didn't use any capital letters in their channel name. See which name is easier to read:

thenomnomtruck

TheNomNomTruck

You'll see this type of single word profile names displayed frequently online so next time you set up a profile, remember to use capital letters for the beginning of each word. And like I explained in setting up a Facebook profile, you should fill out all the relevant information about your channel with a good description, adding a profile image or logo, adding your website address and even your location.

Also important is adding keywords to your YouTube channel. This comes after the description and is used in video searches. For Cheez Philly, I'd add these keywords:

Cheez Philly, Cheez Philly Food Truck, Cheez Philly San Diego, San Diego Cheesesteak, CheezPhilly.com

See how those keywords relate to the truck? They include the name of the truck and location information. But notice the last keyword. I used CheezPhilly.com. This is important to note because I'm going to use CheezPhilly.com as the last keyword in all my video tags.

The first keywords could be any relevant keyword when I add them to my uploaded videos. But I want to make sure I have CheezPhilly.com appear at the end of my keyword list. This creates a consistent keyword tag that repeats throughout my videos. By having CheezPhilly.com as the last keyword, all my other videos will show up in the Related Videos list when the video is done playing. This way, there's more of a chance that the viewer will watch another one of my videos. You can essentially dominate the Related Videos list that shows up on the screen by using this tip. Of course this little trick is more effective when you have a lot of videos uploaded to your channel.

Linking Back To Your Site

In SEO, getting a backlink to your site helps build your authority in the search engines. A backlink is simply a link to your website from an external website. The higher the authority of the external site, the higher your authority becomes and you start rising the ranks of search engines like Google.

In this tip, I'll show you how to get a link back to your site from YouTube which is a very authoritative website.

Whenever you upload a video, you need to add a relevant title, a good description of the video and keywords like mentioned before. All of those should have the name of your truck in there somewhere. But when you type your video description, the very first thing you need to add is your website address before any other text.

This way, your website is the first thing to appear in your description and won't get lost at the end of the text. Also, the description only shows about 2 or 3 lines of text. So if your video description is long, your website address will almost never be seen. Your website address will actually be a clickable link and because it is a live link, it is also a backlink to your site. But it will only be clickable if you type it like in the following example:

http://www.CheezPhilly.com

You have to have the **http://** in front of your website address in order for it to be a live link. Also notice I also used capital letters for the first letter of each word to make it more readable.

Other than what I have just explained, using YouTube videos for marketing is excellent for food trucks! You can also embed these videos easily into your WordPress website. YouTube gives you an embed code and you can also customize it to fit the width of your blog posts. That way, your videos won't be too small or appear so big that they overlap into your sidebar!

The default video size YouTube assigns for the embed code is 560x315. If your blog post is only 450 pixels wide then you're going to have a problem. The video is going to overlap into your sidebar and look like a mistake. When you correctly size your videos, it'll make your website look more professional!

Chapter 10 - Pinterest for Food Trucks

I've talked a lot about the various methods and tools to market your food truck. Some are free while others are inexpensive. In this chapter, I want to talk about Pinterest for marketing your food truck. Pinterest began as a free online scrapbooking service that got a lot of attention by females. Whenever a user found an image they liked on a website, they could "Pin It" to one of their Pinterest boards for sharing. Pinterest is essentially a social network that primarily features images instead of text. If an image is popular, it could immediately go viral by users re-pinning that image.

In early 2012, there were a reported 5 million users on Pinterest with nearly 1.5 million unique visitors daily. Those users spent at least 15 minutes per day on the site. Another stunning fact is that Pinterest drove more traffic to websites than LinkedIn, Google+, YouTube and Reddit combined!

A few businesses might have a hard time finding a connection with Pinterest if there aren't very many visual elements tied to their business but food trucks can definitely take advantage of this popular network.

Remember I mentioned earlier that you should be taking pictures and video whenever you can? Well, those pictures and videos you post to your website can be pinned to your boards. By doing this, you create more backlinks to your site and improve the authority ranking. Each picture on Pinterest is linked directly back to the source!

Before you start pinning images, you should think about the names of different "Boards" you want your images to appear in. A board is basically a category or folder where you will organize your images. Pinterest users can follow one of your boards or all. For Cheez Philly, I could create the following boards:

Cheez Philly

Food Truck Graphics

Street Food

Cheesesteak

Gourmet Sandwiches

San Diego Food Truck

Yum

You don't have to create all your boards at once but you should come up with creative names that draw attention. When you pin a photo, you are allowed to include a description. Be detailed when you add your text.

Effective Pinterest Tips

When you're starting out with Pinterest, you should use your food truck name as your profile name. If you didn't do that, you can change your profile name after your profile is set up. Your profile name will be used in the direct web address to your Pinterest page. For CheezPhilly, the Pinterest page address will be:

http://pinterest.com/CheezPhilly

When you're in the Edit Profile page, be sure to fill out the About section. This text will show up directly under your photo on your Pinterest page. This allows users to learn more about what your business is about and the type of topics you're interested in. Like I explained in the YouTube chapter, you should insert your main webpage address as the very first thing in the About section. Remember the web page address needs to start with http:// for it to be an active link.

Pinterest allows you to connect your Facebook and Twitter accounts with your profile. You should definitely link those accounts. When your accounts are connected, the Facebook and Twitter icons will show up under your profile image that link to those respective pages. There's also the option to automatically publish your Pinterest activity to your Facebook timeline.

You'll need to pin regularly and consistently which can help maximize your exposure to the Pinterest community. You can also add mentions in your descriptions that let others know you've acknowledged them in your pin. When you mention another user, this is what it would look like:

@username

Obviously replace "username" with a valid Pinterest profile name. By mentioning other users, it helps create more exposure while building a larger following for your boards. Its good practice to pin from various sources but you should definitely pin your own blog posts since your objective is to promote your business. This is easy to do if you've installed the Pinterest "Pin It" Button plugin for WordPress. If you have the plugin installed, just click the "Pin It" button that appears on your published blog post to pin to Pinterest.

If you have a YouTube channel, it's a good idea to pin your videos too! While Pinterest is used primarily to pin images, videos can help set you apart from other users. And add keywords to all your pins so they can be easily found in searches.

Who's Pinning Your Stuff?

Sometimes it's useful (or just interesting) to know who is actually pinning your stuff! Here's a handy little link that will tell you just that. It needs to be structured as seen below:

http://pinterest.com/source/yoursitehere

In the example URL, just replace "yoursitehere" with your webpage address. Again, using our imaginary food truck Cheez Philly, this is what the address would look like:

http://pinterest.com/source/CheezPhilly.com

That link is basically a search and will return a page of results that shows you all the images that were re-pinned and show the Pinterest username associated with that re-pin.

Part of a Complete Marketing Plan

Here are some final thoughts on the kinds of boards you can create. You can use your boards to help tell the complete story of your food truck business. With this in mind, you could create individual boards to feature your employees, your truck at different locations, behind the scenes, special events like weddings or other catering jobs, your merchandise, t-shirts and more!

With the growing popularity of Pinterest, a food truck marketing plan would be incomplete without incorporating this powerful social network into your strategy.

Chapter 11 - Using Contests to Gain Massive Followers

I've saved the best for last! This chapter ties together just about everything I talked about in this book. You may or may not have thought about contests but after you read this chapter, I'm sure you're going to think differently about the whole concept of contests. Especially when you hear how easy they are to conduct online.

However, you do have to have a website that is self-hosted and managed with WordPress before you can implement the contest tool for your business. Remember earlier in this book when I talked about needing extra functionality on your WordPress website? Well this is where the premium WordPress plugin called Contest Domination comes in.

Big companies know that running contests can create major publicity and can prompt people to buy their other products and brands. Running a contest like the professionals do costs a lot of money! But if you use Contest Domination, you can run unlimited contests for less than $40 (at the time of this writing)!

Creating Automated Contests

Up to now, individuals and small businesses have run contests on their websites in a very clunky way. Most do it by having website visitors leave a comment on a blog post and when the contest ends, the website owner would have to manually pick winners from a huge list of commenter's names. Announcements of the contest could be posted on Facebook and Twitter. However, the reach of these contest messages were rather limited and had to be monitored.

With Contest Domination, all of that is automated. The contest pages generated by the plugin are gorgeous and the winners are picked automatically when the contest ends. This is all great but there is a lot more to this plugin than just running a simple contest.

This plugin will actually help you generate an explosion of Twitter and Facebook followers. Not only that, Contest Domination will also significantly increase the number of email subscribers on your list! But how is this possible? The developers of this WordPress plugin built in some really great features.

Incentivized Contest Entries

Contest Domination has the ability to generously reward entrants who refer other people. This is how your contest can be spread virally. Entrants are encouraged to share the contest link and to have others submit entries because the original entrant receives additional entries to the contest for each successful referral. This is a huge incentive for entrants to share links to your contest! You can set the number of additional entries a person will get with each referral.

The plugin actually keeps track of the number extra entries a contestant has secured through referrals and they can come back to the contest page to see how many entries they have. This offers proof that their sharing efforts are paying off! Obviously, the more entries the entrant has, the higher the chance of winning.

So Far You've Earned **491** Entries. *get more!*

**Get Your Friends To Enter...
Get More Chances To Win!**

STEP 2: Tell Some Folks!

Share on Facebook: `f Copy`

Share on Twitter: `Tweet`

Share on LinkedIn: `Share`

Share anywhere with this special link:

http://contestdomination.com/?c

STEP 3: Stay in Touch!

Follow   *to see if you win*

Subscribe 12 *to our updates*

There is also the ability to link your contest with social networks to encourage more referrals. The built-in sharing networks include Twitter, Facebook and LinkedIn. Contestants can also make use of a customized URL that has a unique link that tracks entries just for that contestant. This link can be placed anywhere links can be embedded.

Contest Domination also seamlessly integrates with the AWeber email marketing service with a simple drop down menu. This is crucial because for contestants to enter your contest, they need to submit their name and address to you. This adds them as a subscriber to your newsletter and adds them to your email list. With this plugin, you have another extremely effective way to gather massive members to your email list! Can you see how powerful running a contest with this plugin can be?

Think about running your contests at the beginning of your operating season and you'll gain a huge amount of followers right away! The prize you give away could be anything valuable but here are some suggestions.

Free Meal(s)

Free T-Shirt

Free Catering

iPad Giveaway

Guest Chef Opportunity

Private Party

There are numerous things you could give away but the real value in holding contests is to gain more followers and subscribers. That is what will drive more customers to your truck. Use this as a secret weapon to rise above the competition!

Building Beautiful Contest Pages

Creating a contest page is easy. Contest Domination has pre-built templates and all you have to do is input a few details about your contest. Getting the contest up on your website is as easy as publishing a blog post in WordPress. When you're creating your contest page you can upload your logo, link your social media accounts and your email marketing account. An optional image of the prize can be uploaded and inserted into the contest page.

Other details you need to assign are the number of entries each referral is worth, the number of winners per contest and the all-important contest rules. You can save all this information to speed up the creation process if you plan to run multiple contests.

Lastly, you'll need to set the contest start and end times and publish the contest page. At this point, start letting people know about your contest on your social media network and you can watch your follower count increase rapidly!

This plugin is really easy to use and there's no programming involved. When your contest ends, Contest Domination automatically picks the winners. You can then notify the contest winners with the email address they provided. Since this is a contest where people want to win the prize, there's a higher chance that entrants will use their real email address (rather than a junk email address) because they want to be notified if they are the winner. This also means that you're more likely to capture email addresses that are higher quality and can bring you more customers.

As with most software, you can try it out to see exactly how it works with your Wordpress site. You can get a demo copy of Contest Domination at:

foodtruckbusinessplan.com/ContestDomination

I believe this is a tool no food truck owner should be without! Food truck businesses rely heavily on social media and this is the perfect tool to grow your network!

Chapter 12 - Marketing Success!

In this book, I've laid out an effective marketing strategy that is both cost effective and simple to implement! Food truck owners have to be resourceful to keep costs down while finding innovative ways to bring in more customers. A lot of food truck businesses don't have a lot of staff and owners often end up doing most of the work.

The strategies and tools described here are extremely simple that almost anyone can follow. If you're a do-it-yourself type of person, the techniques I described are perfect for you! There are many parts to a good food truck marketing plan. You can implement some or all of the techniques/tools you just read about.

It's not enough to just place Facebook and Twitter logos on your truck and business cards. You need to be active in your social network to engage your audience and let them know what you're all about.

Even if you're not in the food truck business, the techniques explained in this book can apply to almost any business that wants a larger social network of followers. Each person is unique with their own set of thoughts and ideas when it comes to marketing. That's what makes food truck marketing so fun!

Being creative and different is what makes a good marketing campaign.

What can you bring to the table? What are your strengths when it comes to marketing? If you combine your creativity with a good plan, you're bound to find success. Everyone has access to the same tools but the people who put them to good use will usually come out the winner! I hope I was able to enlighten you with new information about how to successfully market your food truck business!

Good luck and I wish you success on the road!

Would You Like to Know More?

Learn more about the food truck industry and what it takes to start your own food truck business with the other titles in the Food Truck Startup series.

The best part is that I frequently run special promotions and discount my books (usually $0.99 USD). It's a great way to save and learn about this unique career path.

The best way to get notified of these deals is to subscribe to my Entrepreneur's Book Club. It's free to join and you'll also get a copy of **Food Truck Vehicles and Equipment**. This free guide will introduce you to some of the components and systems found on food trucks as well as details on the actual vehicles.

Please visit the following URL to get promotion updates and download the free book:

TheFoodTruckStartup.com/free

Did you like this book?

I'd like to say thank you for purchasing my book. My goal is to provide the most complete information about food trucks and the industry. I hope you enjoyed it!

As a favor, I would be grateful if you could take a minute and please leave me a review for this book at the website you purchased it from. Your feedback will help me to continue writing and updating the information about the food truck industry.

Thank you!

Andrew Moorehouse

Blog: FoodTruckBusinessPlan.com

Books: TheFoodTruckStartup.com